THE THINGS THAT ARE

Alice Raphael

THE THINGS THAT

ARE

October House Inc

NEW YORK

Published by October House Inc
55 West Thirteenth Street, New York

Printed in the United States of America

Library of Congress Catalogue Card Number 70–84565
SBN *Cloth 8079–0155–5*
SBN *Paper 8079–0156–3*

To

Mark Van Doren

I

I know that I am mortal and ephemeral; but when I scan the multitudinous circling spirals of the stars, no longer do I touch earth with my feet, but sit with Zeus himself, and take my fill of the ambrosial food of gods.

Ptolemaeus

SONG

Oh, be thou, my ghostly lover,
Consecrate to me,
As I long years
To thee, to thee!
O my Daimon! Despite
Thy volatile inconstancy,
Thou art self-luminous,
Scintilla of light!

Wayfarer, pause
Before this cross-road stone
Where I,
Once Myrrah, lie,
Foredoomed, alone.
Eros came, in silence hushing
Breath with breath;
Later—crushing
Laughter—death.

I was Diotimus of Melos and do not know whether Leonidas the Sailor perished in the Gulf of Argolis. My father often quoted these words of Antipater of Thessalonica: "Not even when at anchor trust the baleful sea, O sailor, . . . for Ion fell into the harbour, and at the plunge wine tied his quick sailor's hands . . . !"

Leonidas leaped with me as our vessel foundered, top-heavy with belly-wide wine jars, narrow at the neck as the waist of a Cretan girl is narrow, her long skirts wide and flaring. Twice I sank, twice rose, each time firmly gripped by Leonidas, gauging the distance to the shore. My eyes, when I could wide-open them, beheld a god gliding above horrent waves spitting at his feet their foam.

And I saw, too, another god, his lifted wand gold-tipped by a flame, and souls were following the flame. Not long after, I joined the throng.

I do not know whether Leonidas reached the coast or, weighted by my body, sank straight as a plummet. For he believed in no gods, yet was an excellent sailor, a brave man and my friend.

PIETA

Were you there, Icarus, in your spirit-sheath when the fisher-folk retrieved your broken body from the sea, were you there when at Cumae they laid it across the knees of Daedalus, who from wax and feathers fashioned wings— his escaping, yours accosting death?

Were you there, Icarus, when, rigid as a venerable stone, Daedalus, gazing upon your not yet faded lips murmured, "My son, my son!"

Excavator of cities beneath the sands, I, Lydia, speak. This empty memorial freed from rubble will yield none other than a name incised in marble, mortal reminder of the Roman who governed Libya, not wisely though well. The sands shifting slowly seawards from the desert erased this outpost of Magna Roma—his ruling passion. I know this to be true who forfeited for his purposes my legacy to time. My first-born perished in outer Gaul, his brother in the mist-lands, a far journey from Lundinium. My youngest did not return from Ethiopia, nome of the Black Magicians. Would he had sought sanctuary in Heliopolis, where from his southernmost temple Apollo lets fly his golden arrow against infamy.

To what end the Lex Romana! To what end Magna Roma!

Hecate, hidden nature of the moon at full, who often lured me from my bed into a night-hushed garden—now of my choosing I immerse myself in your pervasive whiteness.

I hurry to the fringe of the woods; I linger above the meadow, where fireflies flashing subtle lights commune. As in a mirage I see myself alone upon a soundless planet— I who perhaps in sleep once followed in your train, Tri-featured One: Luna, Hecate, Diana.

Harvest moon, suspended low, as if a wine-rose fruit filled with sweet seeds were ripe for a god's plucking, allay our anxiety lest the late summer sun—that earth-scorching enemy—destroy our winter provender.

And Aphrodite rose from her ritual bath once more virgin fair. Robed in the pallia of a girl—yet in her bearing a woman, pursuant to the purpose of the gods—she guided her lazily gliding swans three times the circuit of the sky.

Rootlings in darkness quivered; pale filaments pierced the covering of the earth; small nesting creatures stretched awake. And, beholding the Far-shining One—to Zeus dearest of many daughters—man knew his haunting winter-long fear allayed, his vital essence once more aflame.

Let me not in the after-death life sink into forgetfulness, inert as a stone plummeting into a pellucid lake. Let me resist Lethe.

Divine Mnemosyne, when I come to the place of confrontation—one well-spring to my right, one to my left—reach me a cup of your living waters! May I, upon my upward transit, remember whence I came, whither tending.

Praised be the priest at the crossways who sounds the golden gong! And praised be all emanations, whether they manifest themselves as the black doves of Jupiter or the oracular oaks of Dodona.

No warning gong sounds at the crossways of my life, and I proceed without misgivings. For I have seen, though once only, an incandescence shattering as lightning, a sign more powerful than any oracle—be it of Jupiter or of Apollo even.

Inevitable Atropos, have you mislaid your shears? Sever this subtle filament binding me to one, not of the living, yet in nowise dead. Else, black-robed sister, without your aid, I, who would be companioned with my lambent peers, must in life remain a shade.

That night I walked with cautious tread along the frozen rutted path from house to barn, where my white heifer lay in unremitting pain.

Time and again I took my way from house to barn and barn to house—until in early winter-light I saw the trembling little calf and knew, beyond all cavilling, Lucina came . . . at the hour when divinity and creaturehood conjoined.

He came at dusk, the gentle hour, compelling from the air music of such sweetness that the forest trees—even the unbending oak-trees—turned their leaves towards him, and the small creatures in the brushwood listened, and the dauntless lion, the vicious boar, listening, were subdued.

Do not gainsay me this, who shared at eventide my rice and raisins with a stranger-bird; beside me my white cat, indifferent. Indifferent, too, the house-dog lying prone, watching, without hunting-spirit roused, a slant-eyed rabbit at his ease beneath the apple-tree, refuge from antipathies.

My sleek, black Genius-loci lay coiled in sleep upon the garden stone, summoned from his sunken lying-place by bidding-music heard in Thrace at dusk, the gentle hour.

O thou, my Daimon, nightly crying into the dark,
Recurrent sorrow, voiced in vain,
Speak by day with a god's trumpet voice:

"Wayfarer, overlong becalmed,
Across Pierus blows a ghostly wind:
Land...land!"

Come no further... I cannot say
Whether if I could, I would return;
In this murk of night and day,
My will is a flickering taper-light,
A breath blows away. ... I am adrift,
Lost in mist.

Love, go from me, there is yet time!
Return to the warm earthways
And, upon the breast of a girl
Too innocent to understand,
Dream it is I who sleep with you.

Save for the small flat night-lamp raised above him, deep in sleep,
Save for Venus and her implacable hate,
Would I have brought upon me this corrosive shame?

Blame not the night-lamp nor my caressable hands;
Blame my inquisitive eyes—his wounded faith.
Yet only I, his wingéd girl, can bring to him the lemon-
                            scented balm, steeped in fragrant wine—
Only I, his virgin love, he mine.

Tenor

I am aflame, but not with common fire.
Spirit an incandescence generates
Surpassing kindled light.

Counter-tenor

O Love, clear-running as a gentle spring,
Innocent of source or whitherness,
Rarify desire.

Tenor and Counter-tenor

Into this pure air, scatter stars,
Scatter love with thy giving hands
Across the newly sweetened earth.

Chorus of Boys' Voices

Scatter stars...
      Scatter love...
            Scatter life,
Thou from whom all blessings flow,
Thou, Demeter's little son.

When homecoming to his noble house,
A stranger to the ancient porter's gaze,
I did not question the Wanderer, no, not I,
But went before him up the winding stairs,
Unlocked the tower-room. Below
My hand-maids whispered; one cried aloud
"My lord, my lord!" ... I,
In the highest altitude of Love,
Flung the shuttered windows wide,
Admitting gentle air and Hesperus light.

Surely Eros of the Mysteries, "bearer of bright light and holy," ordained my journey to the Far Isles, borne by a flying whale with fins of silver across invisible seas. Surely Eros, for I came safely to my kinsman.

Although death twice tapped his shoulder and pain was his portion, affirming his manhood he said, capturing my hands, "You are, you know, my Queen." I placed my forehead against his heart in winter-love.

His august hour was at hand. He slipped easily from his earthly shell and strode with re-discovered vigour to the sea, where, sails furled, a vessel waited. Not the young god with flashing wings but Eros of the Mysteries, eldest of the gods, sanctified his journey.

II

Sustaining Love,
Into whose hands I yield myself at last,
Receive me with joy
In this, the hour of the consecration.

May these eyes be touched with the finger of flame
And, knowing divinity,
Peer into the hidels of the heart
With understanding compassion.
Guide these hands
Into the service of beauty
And set my feet
Upon the footprints of thy messengers.

Make of me, Sustaining Love,
Thy sacred amphora.

Light-seed,
Pungent as a grain of salt,
More curative
Than powdered horn
Of the pale Unicorn—
Light-seed,
Enhance thy viable power!
Affirm through me,
Thy Philosophical Tree,
Root, branch and flower.

I would go forth
Clean as a sea-washed shell.
I would go forth
Clear as a crystal bell,
Bright as the shimmering wing
Of a humming-bird moth,
Into my august night.

Afar, at dawn, a voice would sing,
Sweet as a trilling lark
Piercing space:
"Lo, the light!
Beyond it, the dark
Sacred, invious place."

When, at the meridian, the star
Beneath whose influence I came to earth,
Again attained its highest altitude—
At this Prime, I set forth with Soul,
And never cast a single backward glance
Towards the tranquil place where Body lay
Awaiting simple words, God-fearing words,
The same whether to pauper or to prince.

Silently into a soundless world.

Now Soul became an ancient, seasoned guide
Who drew me over a chasm in the dark
I could not cross, transfixed by stark despair.
Peril safely behind me, I perceived
A steadfast light-beam, falling from a source
A measureless farness from the Galaxy,
A measureless height beyond our visible sun.

I sped alone towards this compass-point.

Wisdom comes unproclaimed,
On velvet feet
Softly stepping, as if a discreet
Messenger of the ineffable, unnamed
King were bringing to a hidden friend
A shapely stone,
Talisman to journey's end.

I

And facing the flaming barrier-sword,
Eve said: "Teach me his nature, Lord.
Give me the strength to endure the weight
Of consciousness, outside Thy gate.
Will his appraising eyes of the mind—
Which see me, yet see me not—
Be steadfast, be kind,
When earthbound I suffer my lot?
Lord, thou art far removed, even as he.

Mother of God, clarify me!"

II

"Why," said Adam, "must *I* atone?
Did I seek Thy tree?
Why didst Thou quicken this curious bone
Quiescent in me?
I trod my Path better alone,
Proudly seeking communion with Thee.
Thy solitude—must it be ever re-won?
I, who thought myself somewhat Thy son,
Mistrust this flesh of my soul, this feeling,
Stealthily stealing
To subjugate me. Who is this being?

Cleanse my eyes, Lord, for deeper seeing."

1

Critics are like brushers of noblemen's clothes.
PROVERB

The rain-drops striking with staccato touch upon my window-pane
Sound as innocent of malice as the comments of Tibellus the Critic,
Whose words, however, are not as cleansing.

2

Midnight: Transition to Prime

As when a mother smiles,
Covering her sleeping child
Against the infuriate night
With her fleecy shawl,
I, my spirit-son, sensing you
Within me warm, in a cocoon of love,
Smile, turning to the Light.

III

Let no man protest his end if his orchard ripens, winter rye is harvested, and his son's sons bear witness to their frugal forbears.

But if fruit has shriveled, tares choke the fields, and his son's sons do not attest their heritage—then plangent lamentations will rise from Sheol to haunt his seed.

Whence the decisive voice, who the spokesman for my
soul's reprieve in my long dialogue with death?

I bless thee, hieretic messenger, now that I, at no forbidding
distance see, although afar, Kether, Wisdom's crown.

Unblemished gueredon! Whether I trudged in dark of
moon or torrid sun, yet I strove towards thee, mysterious
Crown.

REBEKAH

And the damsel was very fair to look upon, a virgin,
neither had any man known her; and she went down to the well,
and filled her pitcher, and came up.

GENESIS 24; 16.

Mother, my mother, tell me true,
How shall I know my lord—if he comes?
"Stay, my child, near the drinking well."

The caravans come and the caravans go,
I fill my pitcher time and again,
Yet am alone, at the drinking well.

Mother, my mother, at dusk I knew
My lord had come—for he found me where
I waited at the drinking well.

DEBORAH

Then sang Deborah and Barak the son of Abinoam on that day, saying,
Praise ye the Lord for the avenging of Israel, when the people
willingly offered themselves.

JUDGES 5; 1 and 2

I praise Thee, Lord:
Thou didst not summon me from Deborah,
Who sought from Thee, avenging, ravening power;
No, Thou hast flowered me from viable seed.

And I, who for Love's sake, could forgiving be,
Am from my own root-self redeemed,
Not from the seed of Deborah.
I thank Thee, Lord.

I

Now I beheld Israel restored to its heritage,
And at the gates of Jerusalem I heard a crier by night declaiming:

"Let it be said we are a race of dreamers,
Let the finger of scorn be pointed at our heads,
Let the hands of the nations be raised against us
Until we girdle the earth with the footprints of the exile.
For truly we dream a dream beyond the Imperial,
We who seek a covenant with the souls of those set against us.
Yea, we shall yet make manifest the vision of a race of dreamers:
The world one nation—God, its king."

2

I looked eastwards and heard a crier by day declaiming:

"Do not withhold yourself from the tidings of your generation.
Listen to the voice rising in the soul of the people,
Through the soul of the people speaks the voice of God!

    He breaks the backs of the mighty,
    He forces the bitter cup to the lips of the proud,
    He infuses hope into the veins of the impoverished,
    He raises the strong to the seat of judgment.

O give yourself, give yourself to the creation of a new universe!
Though your limbs sink indolently into flaccid habits,
Though your mind doubts and questions the ultimate issue,
Remember that the final answer is the judgment of your choosing!

    Give yourself with running pride to the soul of the people,
    Listen with joy to the tidings of your generation,
    For your soul answers alone to the voice of its God!"

O passerby, tell the Lacedaemonians that we lie here obeying their orders.
Epitaph of an unknown Spartan
who died at Thermopylae

Now is a darkness falling upon America.
This is the hour when the heart communes with itself.

In my prairie lands, beating hoofs hammer the dry, hot earth,
                              awaiting the fructifying rain!
But there is no health in Manhattan,
No promise of renewal in its sterile soil.
O crafty money-makers, manipulating the nation,
How powerfully you have separated America from the purpose of
                              the Great Spirit,
Confusing the world with the multiplicity of spurious glamour!

Leaderless you charge, past-masters of manipulation,
While the coil of my anger cleaves the air like a lariat!

Let no screen, no curtain upon the stage of history
Cast a flattering light upon the patriots, costumed as officers,
Who crowded the amphitheatre of Washington!
How paltry their histrionics in the light of time!

Speak to me not of the Argonauts! Nor of Theseus!
Tell me naught of the Spartans who died at Thermopylae!
None went more bravely to meet their destiny than did the lads
Whom I beheld marching down a wide brick avenue in the glare of
                              an August noon,

47

Sacrificial offerings to the Spectre of Man,
Whose pinions shadow the land.

Where once the harvesters gave themselves in free-will offering,
Now toilers demand an answer to ultimate issues.
East and West have my daughters taken part in the judgments of the
                                                                nation,
Yet will their victory be to love—or to power?
Where stands the symbol, whose the sign?

> *O mysterious wisdom of Chaldea,*
> *Illumine the mind of Man!*

I

Sophia

No robe, no diadem,
Nor even the lustrous gem
Betokening the soul's estate
Graced Sophia, crouching at the gate
Debarring hope of Paradise.
And Jesus came and Jesus said:
"Sophia, soul of me, arise!
Lest I, without thee, incomplete,
Fail, serving the Paraclete,
Lest man be doomed and I be dead."

II

A Council Meeting

First Elder:
He still is One though He is Three,
And Word made flesh is God-like Man.
He one'd with us; we, striving, scan
The frontiers of infinity.

Second Elder:
The Absolute contains the Good.
And symbol-worship is aligned
To devious depths of human mind;
God need not be understood.

Third Elder:
This life is real and we are far
From certainty of what we are,
Dust or fragmented star.
If we affirm this Threefold sign,
What law will safeguard me and mine
From fate's implacable design?
The graven laws must be our guide.

And Jesus bowed his head and sighed.

III

Viable Error

And Mary—not his earthly mother—said:
"Speak to us of the dead,
  The small dead children, breath denied at birth.
  Are they of heaven? Are they of earth?
  Must this unripened fruit forever be
  Refused Thy ministry,
  Thy firmly planted Tree?
  Air-borne blossoms, thwarted in the seeds,
  Sway in Cosmos, as rootless weeds
  Drift in a shifting sea.
  The decree, the Elders' rigid words,
  Harsh as the cackle of aging birds
  Flays the mute, unreconciled
  Spirits of innocents who await
  Mitigation of unwarrantable fate."

"No sin, but viable error," Jesus smiled.

At last Metatron spoke,
Facing the light.
"Master, is it well?
Silence broods
As a night pregnant with storm,
Yet no word comes.
What then shall we say to the waiting ones?
Their tapers flutter in the ice-wind,
Piercing our ranks,
And from the bowed heads,
Sound creeps towards the shadow of the throne.
Shall we draw nearer,
And bid the day tarry?
Or shall we stoop down in pitying comfort,
Touching the anguished?
For lo, the earth waits!
The yes or no, the end, the beginning—
Now Master, the sign, the sign!"

J. Abelson's Jewish Mysticism *gives a discussion of Metatron, in whose symbolic figure we find the very essence of the Saviour idea. He was considered the angel in whom God's name exists, and thus a kind of essence of the Deity Himself. Intercessory powers were centered in Metatron. A striking passage depicting Metatron, not alone as pleader for Israel, but as taking upon himself the burden of Israel's sins, is found in the Introduction to Lamentations Rabba, xxiv. No sooner was the Temple burnt than the Holy One said, "Now will I withdraw my Shechinah from it and I will go to my former habitation." At that hour the Holy One wept, saying, "Woe is me! What have I done!" Forthwith Metatron fell upon his face, exclaiming, "O Sovereign of the Universe, let me weep, but weep thou not!"*

But the stillness held,
And about the throne
Trembled the Sephiroth,
And murmur sped like a hush to silence Metatron.
Yet he prevailed,
Bowing towards the light.
"Master, behold what they have done,
Blotting thy work,
Blurring the image.
Grain no longer stems the rippled field,
And even the poppy is quelled in the furrow,
Pale beside another red.
And there are no quilted clouds to veil the earth
As the night passes,
But only smoke fretting the dawn,
And smoke clouds the sun's disc,
And smoke presses up to us, shields of Thy Glory,
Shrouding them from Thy sight.
Ah! well it is that they are shrouded!
For the brute creeps out again!
I, hovering above them, know not what to answer;
Is it to be on and ever on again,
Hope playing the whiphand to despair,
Or shall once again come the impenetrable night?
Speak, Master, speak!"

Still hung the silence,
Heavy with the weight of storm.
And now the Sephiroth abashed,
Hid their brightness beneath unfolding wings,
Crouched like grey sea gulls about the throne.

But Metatron drew nearer.
"Behold, Master, the smoke widens,
And there is a lull in the violence,
Until I, leaning down,
Catch a glimpse of their ravished day.
Shadows, shadows fill the lifespan,
And no sun creeps across the heavens,
Save in the memory of happy hours,
Else all is dark.
For what is life to the scorched flesh,
And what is hope to the veiled eyes,
And what is love to the sterile,
Or joy to the devastated young?
Empty lairs are their homes, Master,
As they creep from the soil like whelps,
Who know not their mother again;
Ever on and on they straggle,
For the Mother is dead.
Grey waste has wiped out her joy,
Where the harvest glowed, rich and smiling,
And where the forests breathed her fragrance,
There is but firewood,
And deep within her heart,
Where once her children slept apart in the long silence,
All are now jumbled in hideous disarray."

Then the silence broke suddenly,
And the Sephiroth, trembling in the darkness,
Sped away in horror,
Leaving Metatron.
Now raged the voices of interminable space,

And light played about him and below,
Yet touched him not.
For he alone had dared,
And daring all, dared nothing.
And as he stood with eyes undimmed,
The planets crashed the torrents of their cry;
About him swung the stars,
Lighting the void,
While ever on the moon's dead light skirted the Throne.

Suddenly all was hushed;
Yet from the circle,
No word reached down.
But when he grew near, then nearer still,
He saw the anguish of the understanding heart,
And heard the sound of unavailing tears.
And as they fell, striking Metatron,
He shuddered....

And all that he had heard below,
Rose up a thousand thousand fold,
A thousand times endured.
Then before the all-encompassed sorrow,
He flung himself with supplicating hands.

"Weep not, Master,
But let *me* weep instead!"

Blessed be the Light which led me,
Blessed be the Tree which felled me,
Blessed be the Hands which held me,
Holy the Breath which fed me.